UNDERSTANDING BEREAVEMENT

Professor Ashoka Jahnavi Prasad

Understanding Bereavement in Clinical Practice

by

Professor Ashoka Jahnavi Prasad

DEDICATED TO

MY MENTOR ,PROFESSOR MAX HAMILTON

ACKNOWLEDGEMENTS

I deeply appreciate the help and support of colleagues who worked with me. Thank you for the time you spent with me, revisiting the rich memories of our work.

CONTENTS

INTRODUCTION

How do families grieve when a loved one has died? I learned the answer to the question during 11 years of participation in a unique family---focused bereavement program. I facilitated groups of parents who had lost their spouses. Their children came to the program with them to grieve with other children in their own groups. These parents were young people who lost their spouse or partner long before they should have in the natural order of events. Whether the death was due to illness, accident, suicide or even murder, their lives were upended. They needed comfort. They needed to be with others who had suffered a similar tragic loss. They needed to tell their story. They needed someone to listen.

Companioning is a model in which the grieving person shares the experience of loss, sadness, pain, and heartbreak with others. It is an interactive experience. It is not therapy. There are no rules or protocols. It is in the opening up to an empathic person or a group of caring individuals that the healing takes place. It is fully in the realm of the support group model.

The Den for Grieving Kids (*The Den*) in Greenwich, Connecticut helps children, teens, and their families cope with loss. Divided into age --- appropriate groups, children find comfort in sharing their experience of loss with other children who have had a similar experience. Likewise, adults who have lost a spouse, a partner, or a child join with one another for sharing and support. Telling their story enables individuals in the group to connect at a deep level. Listening is powerful; it is a gift we can offer to people in distress.

The Den operates under the principles of the Dougy Center, a nationally renowned program for grieving children and their families. Core principles are that grief is a natural reaction to loss, the capacity to heal oneself is within each individual, the duration and intensity of grief are unique for each individual, and that caring and acceptance assist in the healing process. At the beginning of each *Den* session, the facilitators recite *The Creed,* which highlights the essence of the program:

"We, the facilitators at *The Den for Grieving Kids,* come together in caring and acceptance to facilitate the healing process of each person who has come here openly and with trust. We accept that grief is a natural reaction to loss. Through listening and sharing, we move toward our goal of personal healing and inner peace. We pledge to honor our process and each other's privacy. It is with this in mind that we begin our evening of healing".

This book will explore the concepts of the companioning model of grief work. Personal stories of families and facilitators will demonstrate the power and effectiveness of this model. The profound effect of losing a parent at an early age will be presented, emphasizing the tremendous value of helping children deal with grief and not repress it. For parents who have lost a child, the tragedy is overwhelming and feelings of hopelessness about ever being able to function normally prevail. The sharing of these horrific tragedies brings strength and hope back to the bereaved parents. The book will present rituals and traditions of *The Den*. Always, respect and confidentiality are guiding principles.

PHILOSOPHY/MODEL

Philosophy of Companioning

Alan Wolfelt, Ph.D., founder of the *Center for Loss and Life Transition,* coined the term 'companioning' for this model of grief counseling. The bereaved person is not a patient who is being treated. Grieving is not an illness. It is not a medical condition that requires a diagnosis and treatment. When we companion the bereaved, we walk by their side, we listen, we empathize, we offer our unconditional love and support. We bear witness to their pain and suffering. We honor their need to tell their stories over and over again; we support them by listening to their stories of love and loss. Dr. Wolfelt distinguishes companioning from a technique or a therapy; it is a philosophy that is ever present in the life of the companion.

There are six key words or phrases that are included in *The Creed,* the statement of purpose of the program at *The Den,* presented in the introduction.   These elements in the companioning model are: caring, acceptance, listening, sharing, personal healing, inner peace. We come to the side of the bereaved with caring and acceptance.   We listen carefully to whatever they say to us.   We share our own stories of grief.   We are equals in the process.   In this way the goal of personal healing and inner peace is achieved. The companioning philosophy of grief care is a shared venture among the bereaved individual, group members, and the facilitator.   We are fully open to one another's experiences and we learn from each other.   A bond is created that facilitates the healing process.

The Meaning of Healing and Recovery

Karen, a grieving mother whose son died, thinks of the medical definitions of healing and recovery: "a return to one's previous state of wellness." For the bereaved, that will not happen. In time they may achieve some state of wellness, but they will never be exactly the same as before the loss. Karen thinks of grieving as a rope that pulls one along. In time, we decrease the tension the rope has on us and we begin to navigate with less pull. Eventually we learn to walk side by side with our grief. It becomes one aspect of our lives, not the total focus. We are able to find pleasure in work and social activities; we can think about the future, but grief is a reality of our lives. Slowly, some semblance of normal life returns. We have a special place in our hearts for the loved one who died; we are always in touch with that special place as we go about the affairs of living. We make grief a part of our lives. We live with it, but do not overcome it.

Facilitators

Who are the facilitators? Who are these people who volunteer their time to companion the bereaved? They are adult men and women from various backgrounds and of a range of ages. There are no formal requirements for participation regarding education or work experience. They are individuals who have the desire to interact with others in a helping and supportive way. *The Den* attracts some people with a mental health background but it is not a prerequisite. Some have had losses in their own lives, resolved or unresolved, which may attract them to *The Den* program. There is an interview and application process. Facilitators make a one---year commitment when they join the program. In most cases, they stay much longer, some for many years. Despite the inevitable ups and downs regarding leadership and administrative changes that any organization faces, the facilitators continue to come, year after year. They come because they believe they are doing important work for the families. They believe passionately in the profound benefits of their companioning the bereaved. Lynne G. says that she has participated in many volunteer activities in her life, but never has she met such dedicated, fine people.

There is a training session which takes place over a
weekend. It is an overview of the program and the role of
the facilitators which involves practice in reflective listening, role
play, background information about the companioning model of
grief counseling and program activities.
Experienced facilitators attend to be helpful and supportive to the
new volunteers.

Alan Wolfelt writes in his book, Companioning the Bereaved: A
Soulful Guide for Caregivers:

> *"My experience suggests that few helping situations*
> *are more challenging—or more rewarding—than*
> *the opportunity to assist people impacted by loss in*
> *their lives. Perhaps through deepening our human*
> *capacity to respond to each other in times of grief,*
> *we can continue to enrich each moment of our*
> *living."*

Most facilitators believe that their work at *The Den* leads to
meaningful personal growth. The work is hard. It is sad yet
it is tremendously rewarding. The companion (facilitator)
connects on a deep level to a person who is hopeless and
despairing by being one hundred percent available to him
and by truly feeling and understanding the pain. This

experience is profoundly fulfilling.   When you try to help
someone heal from her pain, it is likely that you are healing
yourself as well.   Many facilitators say that they have learned to be
 more of a "companion" to their own children and families in
dealing with everyday interactions.   Some   say   that their
companioning work at *The Den* has served to connect them to
their own unresolved grief issues of which they were unaware when
 they joined.

Facilitators find that their companioning work at *The Den*
results in an ability to reach out to bereaved people in their
personal lives.   They have a comfort level in talking about
loss that is not prevalent in the general public.   Helen, a Den
facilitator, was at a pool party one summer afternoon.
Another guest was Maureen, a young woman whose mother
had died unexpectedly a few months before. Knowing
Maureen and her family, Helen had sent a caring condolence
note to Maureen and had received a gracious thank you card.
For most people, that would have been enough.   Why bring
up the death at a fun---filled social event where people were
laughing, talking and having a good time?   get it was natural
for Helen to refer to Maureen's loss, giving her a hug and
engaging her in conversation about her mother.   Maureen
expressed how appreciative she was that the subject was
brought up.   Helen was the only person at the party who had
mentioned it.

The deep satisfaction of such encounters, both outside and within The Den, can result in a profound dedication to the work of companioning

Bonding of Facilitators

An essential aspect of *The Den* companioning program is the bonding of the volunteer facilitators. Facilitators meet before and after the sessions with the families. The first session is called the Pre---Session and the second session is called the Post---Session. The facilitators gather at 5:3f in the afternoon, a half hour before the families arrive. Sitting at a large table, side by side with one or two staff members, they prepare for the evening's work by moving into a relaxed, contemplative mood. The cares of the day and the pressing issues in their personal lives are pushed aside. The room is darkened. Soft music is played as they participate in a few minutes of meditation. Then, a ritual called "Pass the Bear" takes place. A child holding a bear is *The Den's* logo. Holding a stuffed bear, soft and cuddly, each facilitator has an opportunity to share thoughts and feelings with the group on any subject. It can be personal, worldly, humorous, political or focused on a loss in the community or the world at large. The opportunity to passhnot to speakhis an acceptable option.

The rest of the Pre--- Session addresses details of the evening's activities. Facilitators express individual concerns, ask questions, ensure that the necessary materials for the children's groups are available, and get room assignments. As families start to arrive, the Pre--- Session ends. The facilitators greet the families, mingle and chat with them, until the formal program begins.

The purpose of the Post--- Session is to ensure that all facilitators have an opportunity to process their experience of the evening so that they go home with a clear mind and in a stable emotional state. They sit around the table and report back to the group the events of the night's work, one group at a time. Confidentiality is paramount. This session gives them the opportunity to express their own emotions which may have been stirred up during the meeting. A great feeling of warmth and connection is palpable. The evening of healing is over.

GROUPS

Companioning goung Children

Barbara H., a Den facilitator, refers to the grief work at *The Den* as a partnership of the bereaved and the facilitators. She participated in this partnership for a year and learned a great deal about children's feelings. The children she worked with were so brave, so angry, so sad; they were all confused about why this awful thing had happened to them. She talks about a four---year---old child whose experience at *The Den* enabled him to talk, even in the simplest terms, about the death of a parent.

"He and his whole family had been in a car crash and one of his parents was killed outright. He never talked about it. One evening I was sitting next to him, watching him draw on a big sheet of paper. He had a red magic marker and I realized that he was drawing a crude outline of an automobile. Suddenly he grasped the marker in his fist and started to make red dots all over the picture, harder and harder. Then he made red dots on my arm and on his own, then wildly scribbled out the car outline. I said nothing. After what seemed like a long time he looked up at me and said, 'It was a terrible accident." For the first time he had been able to say out loud what he'd been storing up inside. He finally was able to talk about it."

The youngest group at *The Den* is *The Littles* comprised of three---to---five year olds. They have lost a mother, a father, a sister or brother. Often they are confused and uncomprehending about what has happened. They witness the grief of the family members and experience turmoil and disorder in the home. At first, they don't understand why they are at *The Den*. Gradually trust develops and they begin to feel that they are in a safe place where they can separate from their parent or sibling and join the group with the other little children. They know that every other child in the group lost a parent or a sister or brother even though they don't fully understand what death means. The facilitators help the children become familiar with the vocabulary of grief, experiencing emotion and empathy that they will be comfortable using as they become older. They struggle to put words to feelings and needs.

One activity involved making a timelineh"A Map of Our Lives". In a very simple way, the children pinpointed important events, including the death of the loved one, even if they did not want to talk about it. For *The Littles*, it is not always important to say the words. One child drew a picture of her mom who died. She did not write or verbalize the identity of the person she drew. Drawing the picture indicated that she was processing the death.

Grief work with young children is subtle and indirect. They express their feelings through activities such as artwork and building. Often the boys would start to talk while they were building with Legos and blocks. In one activity, the children colored and decorated small boats. Each one was in memory of someone who died. The children placed a candle in the middle of each boat and floated the boats on a big pond. Some boats were painted the color that was the favorite of the person who died or were named after him. One child named her boat the "S.S. Daddy". Little girls love to make memory bracelets from beads, hearts, letters, and colorful designs. These bracelets may bear the name of the loved one and are often given to the mother or older sibling.

Grieving Teens

Teens have a strong desire to fit into their peer group. They don't want to be different. They are uncomfortable with the extra attention they get because they experienced the death of a parent, a brother, a sister. If they are grieving, they keep their feelings inside. They don't want to talk about their bereavement with their friends because they know it would make the friends feel uncomfortable. So they say nothing and the grief simmers within. At *The Den* they can open up and talk. Every other teen in the room has lost a loved one and is dealing with sadness and pain. They feel safe. They share.

Denise, a veteran teen facilitator, says that if you lose a parent as a kid, you're in the club forever. Denise's father died when she was 1f years old. She wishes there had been a family support group for her such as *The Den*. There was a strong ethic in her family requiring all to be strong for their mother and for each other, which left her shut down in regard to her own grief. She has found that her own parental loss as a child enables her to be especially helpful to the teens in her group. A teenage girl, after attending *The Den* for two years asked Denise: "Does it ever get better?" A rich conversation ensued.

Most teens do not come to *The Den* voluntarily. Their parents insist that they attend. After the first session, however, most come back willingly. Many stay for years, and even drop in from time to time when they are home from college or when they feel the need to reconnect. Allison was a teen who seemed to hate being at *The Den*. She exhibited hostile and oppositional behavior there regularly. When her mother gave her the choice of whether or not to attend, she continued to come. Teenagers are not always consciously aware of the value of their support group, but over time, they feel the benefits of it and continue to attend.

Teen siblings participating in the same group at The Den reap the added benefit of learning to share with each other. On a particular night, a new family had joined *The Den* to deal with the death of the mother. The father, John, attended the parent group; the three siblings, Michael, Evan, and Nora went to the teen group. It was most unusual that Denise's co---facilitator was absent that evening and that no other teens attended. A perfect storm. The children's mother had died seven months before. After a short time that night, it became clear to Denise that these siblings had never talked to each other about their mother's death which had happened quite suddenly and under suspicious circumstances. Michael, Evan, and Nora talked with Denise and with each other for an hour, focusing on the complicated emotions with which they were struggling. It was the beginning of a long and fruitful exploration of their grief which still continues.

Often, teen members don't talk at the first session they attend. The evening begins with members of the group taking turns saying their name and who died. The seasoned participants reach out to the new kids, supporting them and encouraging them. Silence is acceptable. They talk when they are ready. There are pads and pens available for writing down a thought or idea before speaking but they go largely unused. Teens like to talk. Not all their conversation is about grief. They reminisce about the good times and revisit happy memories. They talk about other things going on in their lives but always return to grief related issues. Kate has been coming to *The Den* for eight years, starting in the pre---teen group and moving into the teen group. She does not talk much about her mother, who died when she was 11, but she continues to attend on a regular basis. The connection with the others who have the same hole in their hearts is powerful, even without the accompanying conversation.

For the teens as well as all the other groups, they know why they are at *The Den* that Monday or Wednesday night. They know why they are sitting in that room in the quirky brick building on Arch Street. They know that everyone there has suffered a profound loss. They are not alone.

The teen groups are comprised of an eclectic mix of kids—the jock, the pothead, the nerd, the preppy—kids who would not normally socialize with one another in their outside world. At *The Den* they are on a level playing field. It is inspiring to watch their interaction.

Michael facilitated a teen group for many years. When his job required him to move to Paris for a two---year stint, he continued his work at *The Den* via teleconferencing. It was before the days of Skype and Facetime. Due to the time difference, he called in at midnight for an hour and a half session. A cutout of Michael was present at each session and pictures of new group members were sent to him. The kids thought it was very cool and Michael's extremely effective work with his group went on seamlessly from across the ocean.

After formally ending or just drifting away from *The Den*, some teens return to attend a special candle---lighting ceremony which will be described in a later section, or just to say hello. Most of the teens in Michael's group were boys whose fathers had died. In some ways, Michael was a father figure to them. Although Den policy prohibits outside communication between families and facilitators in between Den sessions, years later, Michael would get calls on his cell phone from former teens, then adults, wanting to touch base and say hello. He even received a wedding invitation from a boy he had worked with many years before. The bond was strong. Michael was a devoted facilitator who went to great lengths to maintain continuity with his group.

Other Groups: Middles I and II

There are other age related groups. Middles I is for children in the 6 to e year old range; Middles II is for pre---teens. As the children get older, their grief work becomes more verbal and less activity focused. However, at any stage, rituals and activities are appropriate and promote the grieving process.

Loss of a Child: Special Parent Group

The loss of a loved one is a profound emotional experience, most often a life--- altering one. Grieving the loss of a child is a unique intense experience. Hence, at *The Den*, parents who have lost a child gather in their own group to share their heartbreak and to tell their stories. Many parents who join this group find that it is the only place where they can talk openly and unselfconsciouslyhwhere they know that the others around the table have also lost a child and are there only to listen, to talk and to share the common experience that has changed their lives forever. Some of these parents come to the group for many years. They find comfort. The group experience memorializes their child. The group knows their child intimately. The bond is powerful; the connection to the group brings solace. As group members advance on their grief journey, some see continued group participation as a way of helping other bereaved parents who are starting down the rough road that they have traversed.

Peter and Joanne came to *The Den* when their son, Todd, died at the age of eight. They had another older son. Their grief was enormous and overwhelming. They had no one in their lives to talk to on an ongoing basishno one who was consistently present for them as the group was. They felt loved and cared for when they came to the group. They came to *The Den* for many years, telling their story over and over again. Gaining mastery of the story helps in the healing and it is rare to find a forum for the retelling in one's private life. *The Den* provided just that opportunity. Peter and Joanne had a very hard time moving on after Todd's death. For seven years, they left Todd's room exactly as it was when he died.

As a result of their work at *The Den*, when Todd's older brother married and had a child, Peter and Joanne found pleasure and comfort from involvement in their grandchild's life.

Some people who lose a child experience an intense level of anger and bitterness regarding the loss of their child which prevents them from healing. Their cynicism and blame blocks them from being open to comfort. Henry's daughter, Suzanne, died after all treatment for a fatal illness had been exhausted. He was furious at the total mismanagement, in his view, of Suzanne's case. He blamed the doctors, the hospitals and the medications. He had no faith in people, believing that no one cared for anyone else and that all people act with selfish motives in every life situation. His rage and negativity interfered with his wife's grieving and they left the group without gaining the help they had sought.

Sonia was a grandmother whose daughter, Maria, had died from an overdose of drugs. After her daughter's death, she assumed the responsibility of raising her granddaughter, Lisa. While Sonia grieved for Maria, she was resentful that her daughter "threw away her life" and felt angry that now, in her sixties, she was saddled with the responsibility of raising a child. She had planned these years to be for herself after a lifetime of working and taking caring for others. *The Den* was a place where Sonia could express these conflicting feelings and receive support and understanding.

Parents and Children Grieve Together

A chief feature of *The Den* is that family members join together to grieve. Parents come with children. Siblings come with each other. Many parents express their desire to find help for their child more than help for themselves. In time they come to understand that the way a child grieves is directly related to how the surviving parent grieves. When the parent has difficulty mourning, the child will be held back also. The children see the parent's participation as approval for them to join their group and be receptive to the sharing and expression of feelings that takes place. The parent's approval to mourn, a support given by verbal or non---verbal messages, is essential to the child's successful grieving. When the child sees the parent in a group, talking to others about the loved one who died, feeling supported and understood, he feels validated and supported in his participation in a group of his own peers. Worry and concern about the needs of the grieving child add to the pressure on the parent, but the concerns are intertwined. Children sometimes feel protective of the parent as they grieve. They don't want their own sadness and problems relating to the loss to make it even harder for the parent to carry on. Grieving together helps expose such issues so they can be explored.

When parents come to *The Den* due to the loss of a child, they are in desperate need to express and explore their own grief. They want help for a surviving sibling but the focus is on their own profound sorrow.

Commitment to confidentiality extends to parents seeking information about what goes on in the children's groups. Parents sometimes ask for specific information about their child because most often, children do not tell their parent what transpires in the group. Facilitators may reassure a parent in a general way but they consistently observe confidentiality. Parents may see the product of an activityh something the child has createdhbut facilitators do not share details of group interactions. Exceptions are made for risky situations where intervention is deemed necessary.

School Groups

One important expansion of *The Den* program came when facilitators realized that there were grieving children who would not be able to come to *The Den* due to transportation or family difficulties. In response, *The Den* program expanded to some local schools. The same philosophy, that of companioning the children who had lost someone very close, carried over to the new setting using different parameters. Trained Den facilitators go to the participating schools to meet with the bereaved students. This requires parental approval and cooperation from the teachers as the children are taken out of class to attend the program. The school facilitator does not connect with the child's family. The privacy issue is different because the children in the bereavement group mingle and interact during the school day with other students who did not suffer a loss. The students in the bereavement group are known by other children and teachers at the school to be kids who have lost a parent or a sibling. At *The Den*, the children have all experienced the death of a loved one. In both kinds of groups, grieving kids coming from diverse backgrounds and who are unlikely to socialize outside of the group are brought together. The fact that the program is successful in both settings underscores the universality of loss and grief and how comforting that shared experience can be.

School groups have the advantage of having systems in place for follow---up when needed. Benny witnessed his brother being murdered by someone he knew. His mother was in drug rehabilitation; his divorced father was an alcoholic. Benny had no family support and no network of any kind. He was an exceptional 12 year---old. Cathy, his facilitator, said he was a boy with "brains and a heart". The group and the school created a safety net for him; they became his advocate. Cathy believes that the school group saved him.

IMPORTANCE OF RITUALS

Opening Circle

The families have gathered. The evening of healing begins with a powerful ritual. They greet one another and engage in small talk and pleasantries. Then they are asked to form a circle, with the facilitators and administrators. Everyone holds hands. One by one, each person in the circle says his or her name, says the name of the loved one who died, and specifies the relationship. For example, "My name is Jessica and my father died." One always has the right to pass and not say anything. The facilitators and administrators also speak of a loss they had suffered; or they may choose to pass. The room is still. The voices are loud or softhe voices of children, of teenagers, of adults,--- often filled with emotion. For the very newly bereaved, standing in the circle and reciting the name takes great courage. It is a first act of reaching out to others and being receptive to their help. For many children, it is the first time they have said out loud that someone diedhtheir father, mother, sister, brother. They realize for the first time that others have suffered a devastating loss and they are not alone. For those who are further along on their grief journey, saying the name is comforting. They have recited the name many times and feel as though others know the loved one and what he meant to them. The large group then breaks out into smaller groups of children, parents, and spouses for the main part of the session.

In some of the smaller groups, there is another opening circle comprised of only the members of that group. Here is another opportunity, in a more intimate setting, for someone to say who died. In a middle school group, Tim never said who died in either the opening circle or the smaller group circle. He always said, "I pass." A new boy, Alex, joined the group and he, too, kept saying, "I pass." One evening, in the small group circle, Tim said, "My little sister died." When it came to Alex's turn, he said, for the first time, "My mother died." The children have a sixth sense about helping each other. Tim knew just how Alex felt and thought that if he, a seasoned group member, would say who died, it would help Alex be able to say it too.   That was a turning point for both boys.

Other Rituals

Rough Rock, Smooth Rock

At the first *Den* session for a family, each member is given a rough, heart shaped rock, symbolizing the rawness of the person's grief.   This event takes place during Opening Circle. The rock is handed to the recipient by a facilitator or member of the group that the person will be joining.

When a family is ready to leave *The Den*, a similar ritual takes place but now the rock is smooth, symbolizing the healing that the family members have experienced.

Memory Box

A shoebox or any cardboard box can be used for a child to decorate with pictures of the person who died.   Photographs may be used or the child can draw pictures and write words associated with her loved one.   The child is encouraged to be creative. Over time, the child fills the box with objects that connect her in some way with her loved one—a comb, a book, a candy wrapper, a t---shirt. Talking about the objects and showing them to others in the group may trigger feelings, both happy and sad, which the child now has the opportunity to express.

Memory Meal

Once a year, the families and facilitators gather for a "Memory Meal" that takes place at the beginning of the evening before the break out groups. All participants bring a food or drink that reminds them of the loved one who died. The buffet table is laden with wonderful dishes and a warm, positive aura is felt. As the meal is being enjoyed, people talk informally about the special food and its connection to the loved one. Betsy, a facilitator of a school group, prepared a memory meal for her group. She asked each participant to talk about a particular food that was a favorite of the person who died. She lovingly prepared these foods and presented the group with a delicious "Memory Meal" that was a catalyst for meaningful conversation about the loss. Dylan had told Betsy that his father's favorite dessert was crime brulje. A little taken aback at the idea of making an exotic dish, which she had never done before, she moved full steam ahead, finding out how to do it, borrowing a particular implement, and presented it to Dylan.

At *The Den* and in the school groups, a safe environment is created in which children and adults can participate in activities that help them to grieve. Food, aromas and memories, both happy and sad, help in the process.

Craft Projects

Facilitators use other tactile and sensory projects to stimulate expression of feelings regarding loss. Doris facilitated an activity in which the children made throw pillows from quilted pieces of clothing that belonged to the loved one who died. Some children spoke of not wanting to wash the pillow for fear that the scent of the loved one would disappear. One girl in Doris' group brought in a heart made of felt and implanted it deeply in the pillow that was made of her brother's shirt. The other children watched. No words were necessary.

Candle Ceremony

This annual event was one of the most moving and emotional that I experienced at *The Den*. A white candle is designated for each family member who died with the person's name on a label on the side of the candle. A large, rectangular shaped sandbox is placed at the front of the room. Families,
facilitators and Den staff gather together, some sitting, some standing, usually in family groups. The lights are dimmed. The names of all those who died are inscribed in a beautiful book that is a *Den* treasure. On this night, as each name is read from the book, a family member lights the candle bearing the name of the loved one and places it in the sandbox. The room is silent. The candles flicker. Tears flow. Memories of those who died flood the room. We are present for each other's pain. When the ceremony is over, we proceed to our groups to continue our evening of healing.

Annual Picnic

In June, all families, facilitators and *Den* staff join together for a picnic on the playground behind the building. It is strictly social --- a time for all to have an opportunity to visit before we start the abbreviated summer schedule. People bring their favorite dishes, the children have their faces painted and swing from the monkey bars. It is a happy event where feelings of loss are pushed aside for a few hours. We have a chance to talk to families from other groups whom we don't know as well and we bond on a different level.

Closing Song

The large group joins together again for the closing ritual of each evening of healing. Everyone joins hands in a big circle --- children, parents, facilitators and administrators --- and with the accompaniment of a CD, we sing "Lean on Me" by B. Withers:

> *Sometimes in our lives, we all have pain We all*
> *have sorrow.*
> *But, if we are wise,*
> *We know that there's always tomorrow.*

CHORkS:

> *Lean on me, when you're not strong*
> *And I'll be your friend, I'll help you carry on. For it*
> *won't be long, till I'm gonna need Somebody to lean*
> *on.*

*Please swallow your pride, if I have things You
need to borrow.
For no one can fill those of your needs That
you won't let show.*

*You can call on me brother when you need a hand, We all
need somebody to lean on.
I just might have a problem that you'll understand. We all
need somebody to lean on.*

CHORkS:

*Lean on me, when you're not strong.
And I'll be your friend, I'll help you carry on. For it
won't be long till I'm gonna need
Somebody to lean on.*

*If there is a load you have to bear That
you can't carry
I'm right up the road, I'll share your load If you
just call me...call me
If you need a friend...call me
If you need a friend...If you ever need a friend Call
me...call me...*

This singing in unison has a powerful emotional effect. We focus on the meaning of our gathering. We recognize that each person in the room is a friend to the others, willing to reach out and to help. We gaze around the circle and see people in pain --- people of different ages and ethnicity, of varying social and economic backgrounds. We know we have a common bond; we have lost someone we loved and who was important in our lives. We are here to share our experience of loss and to help each other heal. We feel a sense of comfort as we end the evening of healing.

Closing Ritual

The Den emphasizes the importance of families having a formal ending to their participation. It is called closing. They are urged to come to their last session and to experience the closing ritual. The ability to terminate shows mastery of loss. However, many families find it hard to say goodbye, even when they are doing well, and just drift away over time.

SPECIAL TOPICS

Reactions to Expressions of Sympathy

Although grieving people appreciate the expression of sympathy, whether written or verbal, they often complain that people don't get it --- they don't truly understand what the bereaved person is experiencing, and so they are perceived to be insensitive. The bereaved feel a distance from the everyday world around them.   Everything sounds muffled; words spoken in kindness don't resonate. There is an unnatural separation between the grieving and those who don't understand grief. An example of a supportive condolence message is expressed in the following communication written to a woman who lost her only brother:

> "We live and die, some days are worse than others, but I hope his memories give you comfort some of those days. I hope you feel him over your shoulder when you need him most. Seven years is not long at all. Sometimes I think we miss our loved ones more each year. We just get used to it and hide it better as time goes on. I just wanted you to know, I hear you. I feel for you, and I know that grief is a life long experience. gou have every right to be full of gloom and doom some days. gou cannot always be positive. It would be nice if we could, but we are human."
> Amy L.

People living without grief struggle to know what to say to the bereaved and what to do to help them. They feel uncomfortable. Sadly, because of this discomfort, after the initial, obligatory communication, they tend to keep their distance. They stop calling and stop visiting, resulting in the further isolation of the grieving person. Over and over again, I listened to women and men tell of their disappointment in family members and close friends who had let them down. In the days and weeks immediately following the death, these friends had made heartfelt pledges of support --- to visit, to spend time with the kids, to take the boy to a ball game, to help with carpooling and babysitting --- but these promises were not fulfilled. For the family members, this is another kind of loss.

The bereaved struggle with the expectations of others which make them feel burdened and angry. As time goes by, many people think that the bereaved person should get on with his life --- put it all behind him and move on. Initially, people may feel sympathetic, but they have their own timeline for when your grieving should diminish and then be over. Such demands are difficult for the bereaved who do not have a timeline for grieving, who take one day at a time and never know what that day will bring in terms of their grief. It has been said that grief is like a one---way window. gou can see others but they can't see you. Often they don't want to see you and will pretend not to notice you because they feel anxious and don't know what to say. gou feel invisible to others. It's hard to understand how the world can go on when your own life has stopped.

Brian W. said, "I think the best, but perhaps most difficult, thing people can do is to try to put aside their own notions of what a grieving person should do for themselves. When my grief was brand new I found I had no time for well--- meaning people who made me feel I should act a certain way or do certain things. Trying to fulfill their expectations took energy from me, energy I couldn't spare. In my case, I was most comforted by those who could drop their own expectations and were willing to just be there with me or for me. That increased my strength. I don't think I could have been 'helped' at that time, but I was very warmly supported by many kind friends."

<u>Cultural Differences</u>

The way one grieves varies from one culture to another. Cultural perceptions and traditions can interfere with grieving. In Asian families, the concept of attending a group with strangers and sharing personal issues is uncomfortable and unacceptable. A Japanese---American couple, Aki and his wife, Mari, came to *The Den* when their 11---year---old daughter died very suddenly. Mari stayed only a short time but Aki stayed for many years, healing and reaching out to others to help them from his own experience. Members of his extended family were not supportive of his faithful attendance. They did not approve of his sharing his personal life with strangers. However, Aki felt passionate about his experience of grieving at *The Den* and benefited greatly from his long---term participation.

Holidays

Holidays are difficult and painful for grieving families. The first Thanksgiving, the first birthday, the first Christmas without the loved one is approached with dread. There is no right or wrong way to deal with these situations; there is only what feels comfortable for each family. Some families do not want to attend a holiday gathering because they think it will be too distressing. They feel a sense of despair and of being out of step with the world. How can they participate in the upbeat and happy activities when their personal world is dark and bleak? When families communicate that they are not planning to attend the holiday event, they are faced with relatives and friends pressuring them to come.

Many families gather to celebrate a holiday, placing an empty chair at the table for the loved one who is not present. At some large gatherings where place cards are put at each person's seat, a place card for the person who died is put at the center of the table.   Some families who dreaded the holiday find that it wasn't too bad --- that the other guests were kind and compassionate in an appropriate way. Other families choose not to talk about the loss at the holiday gathering and just soldier on. One girl told her group, "We don't talk about my dad; it makes my mother too sad." Talking about the person who died may be upsetting but will often lead to laughter and happy memories.

It is wise to involve the children in the planning of the holiday celebration.   Everyone feels better knowing what is going to take place.   It is helpful to kids if they are warned that this holiday is going to be different.   Its rituals and traditions may not be the same without the one who died.   They need to know that their parent may get upset or feel angry or sad and that they themselves may experience distressing moments. They need to be reassured that this is acceptable. Afterwards, it can be helpful to talk about how the gathering went, what felt good and what felt bad, and what to do differently next year.

<u>Emergency Losses</u>

The Den reaches out to the community in trauma situations. In the years I was there, there were several horrific accidents involving the death of a child in local schools.   In such cases, experienced *Den* facilitators volunteered to help the teachers and administrators in dealing with grief and trauma affecting the student body.

The Den responded to the tragedy of e/11 by establishing a special program to companion families who lost loved ones. A decision was made to form groups specifically for the e/11 families rather than to integrate them into the existing groups. As a facilitator of a e/11 group, I considered it a privilege to reach out to these families who were devastated and shell shocked. They needed to talk. They needed to connect to other e/11 families. They needed to tell their stories over and over again and *The Den* gave them those opportunities.

Other Programs

There are other centers and programs throughout the country that use the companioning model. Some, like *The Den*, are directly modeled on the Dougy Center plan or another established program using this model. Other groups adhere to the same principles without actually identifying their model as companioning. Whatever name is applied, the basic principle is that the bereaved person has a companion --- a witness --- as he undergoes his experience of grieving for a loved one. He is not alone. He is in the company of others who have lost a mother, a father, a wife, a husband, a child. He is walking by the side of a companion who shares his anguish at the deepest level.

Circle of Tapawingo is a camp for girls between the ages of nine and 17 who have experienced the death of a parent. It is a free week of overnight camping during which the girls experience typical activities --- sports, swimming, dramatics, campfires, arts and crafts. Woven into the camping experience is the opportunity to bond with other girls who have also lost a parent, to talk about their loss and how they feel about it. For many of the girls, it is the first time they ever speak to anyone about their grief. James L., a volunteer at Circle of Tapawingo since its inception, says, "The magic is that the girls talk to each other. The loss is the common denominator; that is the power".

The adults who work with the girls at Circle of Tapawingo are all volunteers except for a social worker who guides the grief related part of the program. When Circle of Tapawingo first started, the emphasis was on the gift of a week of camping in a beautiful Maine setting. It was an opportunity for the girls to be carefree and to have fun without the heavy burden of their loss being a part of their everyday lives. There was always "circle time" in each bunk, a time during which the girls sat in a circle with their counselors and shared. No one ever had to speak if she didn't want to, but most of the campers did offer their thoughts and feelings about their loss. As time went by, the program evolved to include more grief--- related activities, always subtly integrated in to the general camping program.

A note of thanks from a parent states:

> "There was a moment when everything in our world changed forever. I couldn't believe there would ever be smiles and laughter again. There are tears as I write this, not of grief, but the tears of relief and happiness I feel every year when you reach out to my daughters and give them the gift of Circle of Tapawingo".

The girls often feel transformed by their week at camp. A camper refers to Circle as her second home.

> "It's a place where I'm not afraid to express my feelings and be judged. Everyone accepts you for you and is always there to listen and give advice. We all have experienced the death of a parent, which makes my friendship with the girls here so much stronger. I trust them more than anyone, and we have memories that will last us a lifetime."

CONCLUSION

Companioning the bereaved is a unique and highly personal experience. The companion and the bereaved are equals, not therapist and patient. Connecting to the companion and the sharing of thoughts and feelings, however painful, enable the bereaved to process their grief. They feel honored and respected in a safe environment. The companions experience reward and fulfillment in relating to the bereaved on such a deep level. The observance of rituals, such as the Opening Circle, provides a rich opportunity for all members of *The Den* family to connect with one another. I consider my years at *The Den* among the most important and meaningful experiences of my life.